A New True Book

AZTEC INDIANS

By Patricia McKissack

CHILDRENS PRESS™

CHICAGO

Pyramid of the Sun

O CREDITS

hard Brucker—8 (bottom right), 19

Finders:
ata—17 (left)

ical Pictures Service, Inc., Chicago—
4, 7, 14 (right), 43

Nawrocki Stock Photo:
©D.J. Variakojis—2, 8 (top right), 10,
17 (right), 28, 44 (right)
©Jim Whitmer—12 (right)
©Jeff Apoian—45 (center and right)

Odyssey Productions, Chicago—Cover,
8 (left: top and bottom), 12 (left), 14 (left),
15, 16, 21, 22, 24, 26, 27, 30, 33 (2 photos),
34, 35, 36, 37, 38, 40, 44 (left)

Peabody Museum, Harvard University—45
(left)

Cover: Diego Rivera mural of Tenochtitlán,
ancient Aztec capital

Library of Congress Cataloging in Publication Data

McKissack, Pat, 1944-
   Aztec Indians.

   (A New true book)
   Includes index.
   Summary: Discusses the Aztec Indians, their history,
religion, language, customs, and final days.
   1. Aztecs—Juvenile literature. [1. Aztecs. 2. Indians
of Mexico] I. Title.
F1219.73.M38 1985   972'.01   84-23142
ISBN 0-516-01936-8   AACR2

TABLE OF CONTENTS

Spain Comes to Mexico. . . 5

The Rise of the Aztec. . . 9

Religion. . . 16

Language, Counting, and Calendar. . . 18

The People. . . 23

Everyday Life. . . 32

Merchants, Craftsmen, and Nobility. . . 36

Arts and Sciences. . . 39

The One Who Speaks. . . 41

The Final Days. . . 42

Words You Should Know. . . 46

Index. . . 47

Hernando Cortés kneels before Montezuma, the Aztec king.

SPAIN COMES TO MEXICO

The Aztec Indians
believed that one of their
gods had white skin and a
beard. This god sailed
away on a raft made of
snakes but promised to
return. In 1519 Montezuma II,
king of the Aztec, was told
that white-skinned, bearded
men were coming.
Montezuma believed the
Aztec god had returned.

At first the strangers
were welcomed. Soon,

however, Montezuma
learned that their leader,
Hernando Cortés, was not
a god. He and his men
had come to conquer the
New World for the king of
Spain.

The Aztec greatly
outnumbered the 503
Spanish soldiers. But their
bows and arrows were no
match for Spanish cannons
and crossbows. After many
battles, the Aztec were

An early Aztec drawing shows the power of the Spanish soldiers.

defeated on August 13, 1521.

Who were these people the Spaniards called the Aztec?

Objects found in or near Mexico City—a stone head, two stone structures,
a piece of pottery—give clues to Aztec way of life.

THE RISE OF THE AZTEC

What we know about the Aztec comes from three sources: Aztec "picture books," diaries and records kept by the Spaniards, and objects found by archaeologists.

Humans lived in Mexico as early as 11,000 B.C. Indians wandered from north to south looking for food. By 6500 B.C. many of the Indians had settled in the Valley of Mexico.

MEXICO

Spanish landing places

Tenochtitlán

AZTEC EMPIRE

A carved boulder at La Venta stands as a reminder of Olmec art.

Some of the early Indians were the Olmec, the Zapotec, the Maya, the Toltec, the Mixtec, and the Chichimec. Most were farmers. Their main crop was maize (Indian corn).

About A.D. 1200 the Tenocha people moved into the Valley of Mexico. After many battles with their neighbors, they settled on an island in the middle of Lake Texcóco— "The Lake of the Moon." From this island they built the powerful nation the Spaniards called the Aztec.

Aztec history records it differently.

The image of the eagle and the snake that guided the Aztec to a new land today appears on the flag of Mexico and important buildings.

According to one Aztec legend, a sun god named the Hummingbird Wizard told the Tenocha people to leave Aztlan, their homeland, in 1168. The god told the Tenocha to stop when they saw an eagle eating a snake while sitting on a cactus with red, heart-shaped fruit on it. They reportedly saw this sight on an island in Lake Texcóco. And that is where they settled.

The early Aztec people built a temple to the Hummingbird Wizard. They added to this temple five times—each time making it larger.

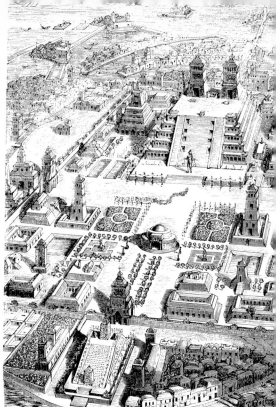

Many artists try to show how the great capital of Tenochtitlán (tay • NAWCH • tee • TLAHN) would have looked during the great Aztec empire.

The Aztec capital was Tenochtitlán. The city was rich with gold, silver, and rare jewels. The great temple and the king's

A scale model of Tenochtitlán has been made at the Museum of Anthropology in Mexico City.

palace were splendid
buildings.

The Aztec nation lasted
from 1215 to 1521. The
kings ruled about 11
million people.

RELIGION

The Aztec had nearly one thousand different gods, but they were mainly sun worshipers. Aztec priests offered human sacrifices to keep the sun god happy.

There were hundreds of priests and priestesses.

A sun altar of enemy skulls was placed near every Aztec temple. The Aztec believed the sun fought darkness every night, but rose each morning to save mankind.

Two of the many Aztec gods that were part of their religious beliefs.

They led hundreds of rituals. They predicted the future and acted as doctors. They also taught counting, writing, science, history, art, music, and dance.

LANGUAGE, COUNTING, AND CALENDAR

The Aztec borrowed Nahuatl, their language, from the valley Indians. But the Aztec were the first to write the language.

Like the Egyptians, the Aztec used pictures to represent words. For example, a foot meant travel. The Aztec wrote about their history, religion,

Aztec picture writing recorded history and business and religious information.

and daily life. They also
wrote poetry. Unfortunately,
the Spaniards destroyed
many of their books.
Today, only a few remain
in museums.

The Aztec had a counting system. Dots represented numbers from 1 to 19. A flag was number 20, a feather was 400, and a bag was 8,000.

The Aztec people had a 360-day calendar. It had eighteen parts with twenty days each. The five extra days were called "empty days." On those days all work stopped. No fires were made. The people

The Great Calendar Stone contained the days of the Aztec year. It also foretold solar eclipses and a great earthquake.

fasted. At the end of the five days, the Aztec priests made a human sacrifice; new fires were lit. Life and the calendar began again.

This famous mural by Diego Rivera shows how three classes of Aztec people lived.

THE PEOPLE

The Aztec had three social classes: the nobility, the merchants and craftsmen, and the peasants.

The Aztec had slaves who could buy or earn their freedom. The children of slaves were born free.

Most of the people were farmers who lived in family units. These units were parts of larger groups called clans.

Detail by Diego Rivera shows clan members building Tenochtitlán.

Each clan had its own leaders, judges, local priests, and schools. Land was owned by the clan.

A clan member was expected to serve in the army or work on building projects. Men who proved themselves in war, excelled in a craft, or served the government well could rise in the social order. Talented girls could become wives of the noble class.

Peasant women made family clothing using a coarse, colorless cloth made from the agave plant. Peasant men wore a white cloak, tied over the right shoulder, called a tilmantli.

A scale model of the Aztec market place is on exhibit at the Museum of Anthropology in Mexico City.

Peasant women dressed in ankle-length skirts and blouses. Sandals were worn only on special occasions.

Merchants, craftsmen, and the nobility tied their tilmantli under their chins.

Diego Rivera mural of Indian headdresses

They also decorated their clothing. Upper-class men and women wore fine jewelry, feathered headdresses, and sandals made from jaguar skins.

Aztec priests wore black hooded cloaks.

The birth of a baby was a joyful occasion. Clan members brought gifts. Girls were named after flowers, birds, or something pretty. Boys were given powerful names taken from nature.

Young dancers perform the traditional dances of their ancestors at the Fiesta San Miguel, San Miguel de Allende, Mexico.

Each clan had two schools called "Houses of Youth"—one for boys and one for girls. Children began school at age three.

The schools were strict. Boys learned citizenship, religion, dance, music, crafts, history, and warfare. They stayed in school until they married and began farming. If they showed promise, they were sent to the capital to study under

Today, people enjoy seeing the Ballet Folklorico of Mexico perform ancient Aztec dances.

the high priests. Ordinarily this was the privilege of the noble class.

Girls were taught crafts, songs, music, art, healing arts, dance, and history. Often they, too, were sent to school in the capital.

Boys usually married at age twenty, girls at sixteen. The parents made all the arrangements. A priest studied the "signs" to see if the marriage would be a good one.

The marriage ceremony was simple. The bride and groom tied their shirttails together. This "tying of the knot" was supposed to bind the couple together for life. Commoners had only one wife; nobles could have more.

EVERYDAY LIFE

Peasant houses were made of reeds and mud. Inside, the one-room, windowless house was divided in two—the kitchen and the sleeping area.

Houses of the wealthy were larger and made of dried brick called adobe.

The Aztec ate corn cakes, beans, sweet potatoes, avocados, squash,

Nobles, slaves, warriors, farmers, and traders crowded the busy Aztec markets.

peppers (chilis), fish, fowl, deer, turkey, and dog. They also ate popcorn!

Aztec peasants grew most of their food. They traded for other things in marketplaces.

Men and boys hunted with blowguns, spears, clubs, and rocks.

Everybody worked from dawn until dusk. Work was done without the help of animals. Although the Aztec knew about the wheel, they didn't use it.

The Aztec worked without the help of animals.

Statue of an ancient Aztec god, Tlaloc, stands outside the Museum of Anthropology.

Like everything in Aztec life, their sports and games were connected to religious festivals. The most popular sport was like basketball. Children played board games, hide and seek, running games, and tag.

An Aztec temple vase being restored

MERCHANTS, CRAFTSMEN, AND NOBILITY

Merchants traveled to far-off places to bring back goods the people needed, such as cotton, cacao, rubber, jade, pottery,

Montezuma's headddress

feathers, nuts, herbs, and medicines. They sold fun items, too. Chicle, for example, was very popular. From chicle the Aztec made chewing gum.

Aztec craftsmen made jewelry, pottery, metalwork, and feathered headdresses. Many served the king as architects and engineers.

Diego Rivera mural shows Aztec nobility in headdresses.

Aztec nobility was the ruling class. Among them were local clan leaders, district leaders, judges, public officials, tax collectors, military captains, record keepers, priests, and advisers to the king.

ARTS AND SCIENCES

Aztec dancing, singing, music, and poetry were part of all religious festivals.

The Aztec made music with flutes, drums, whistles, and rattles. Often during a ceremony the priests would chant this poem:

...Here we come to meet;
We are only passersby on earth.

Aztec artists sculpted in stone, rock, crystal, turquoise, and jade. They painted murals on indoor

and outdoor walls. They worked in clay, gold, and silver. Religious subjects were Aztec themes. Their love of nature also was shown in all their art.

The Aztec used herbs and roots to heal.

THE ONE WHO SPEAKS

The Aztec kings were "elected" for life by a council of high officials. The king was head of both Aztec religion and Aztec government. "The One Who Speaks" was the king's official title, for he spoke for all Aztec people.

The king listened to his advisers. He took tribute (taxes) from conquered nations. He approved or rejected building projects.

THE FINAL DAYS

Montezuma II had ruled for sixteen years when Hernando Cortés landed.

Montezuma's priests reported bad signs in the heavens. To the priests these signs meant doom. When Montezuma heard that white men were coming, he sent gifts of gold and silver, hoping they would take it and go away. Once the Spaniards saw the riches, nothing

Montezuma was killed on June 30, 1520.
Some say he was killed by his own people.

could turn them back. They were determined to see more. And the rest is history.

The Spaniards destroyed the capital and took most of its wealth back to Spain. Montezuma was killed. The Aztec became Spanish subjects.

Left: Archaeologists have found Aztec ruins in the Zocalo area of Mexico City.
Above: Aztec serpent sculpture

Three hundred years after Spain conquered Mexico, the new Mexican people fought and won their independence.

Today, Lake Texcóco has dried up; the great temple of the sun is buried under modern Mexico City.

But there are still Aztec Indians living in Mexico. They still speak Nahuatl, the language of their ancestors, and they continue to make outstanding contributions to the arts, sciences, and culture of Mexico.

WORDS YOU SHOULD KNOW

ancestors(AN • sess • terz) — early family members, usually those who have been dead for many years

archaeologists(are • kee • AHL • uh • jists) — people who study very old objects, buildings, ruins, etc., to learn about the ancient people who used them

clan(KLAN) — a group of families living and working together

cloak(KLOHK) — a loose piece of clothing, often reaching the floor, and usually fastened at the neck or shoulders

conquer(KONG • ker) — to win or defeat, usually by the use of weapons

council(KOWN • sil) — a group of people, usually elected or appointed, that gives official advice, chooses leaders, passes laws, etc.

craftsmen(KRAFTS • men) — people who create things by hand, especially useful and beautiful things

crossbow(KROSS • boh) — an arrow-shooting weapon that has a bow fastened crosswise to a long wooden stick

human sacrifice(HYOO • min SACK • ruh • fice) — the killing of a human in a religious ceremony, often to show respect or fear toward some god

merchants(MUR • chents) — people who buy, sell, or trade

nobility(no • BILL • it • ee) — those of the upper or ruling class in certain countries

peasants(PEZ • ents) — people of lower class, often uneducated, who farm or work for those of the upper class

ritual(RICH • oo • ill) — a ceremony acted out by following certain social or religious rules

temple(TEM • pil) — a building in which religious ceremonies are held

tribute(TRIB • yoot) — the payment of money or valuables by a conquered nation to the government of the conquering nation